Family Ties Sequel

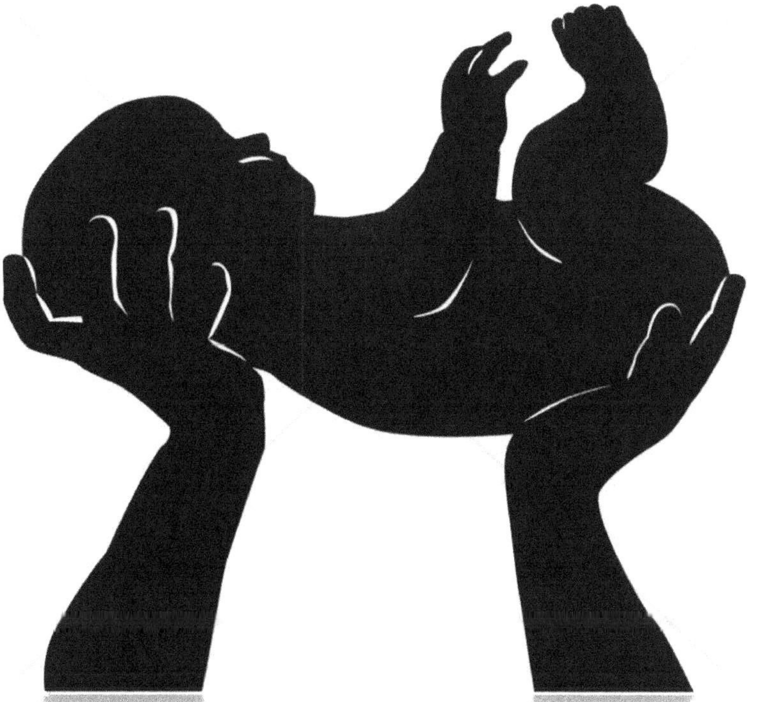

Nikki Nicole

Paperback Edition June 2023

ISBN

Published by Amazon Kindle Direct Publishing

Library of Congress Literary of Works has been applied for

INTRODUCTION

Have you ever yearned for a relationship with your family or wish you still had family reunions to fellowship with your family? It seems like when the matriarch of the family passes away, families stop gathering for events and the only time they see each other is when someone dies. Family means more to me than the word itself. I cherish all my family and I am grateful to be connected to them. Family Ties Sequel is a collection of sentiments withheld and tucked away about loneliness, sadness, happiness, and gratefulness.

You will travel through the halls of sentiments withheld for years, but finally coming to the light.

DEDICATION

It all started with a little girl with the biggest smile and sweetest personality meeting her Auntie for the first time. From the moment I became her Auntie I knew she was going to be great. She is the most intellectual, strong-willed, good-hearted, and diligent woman that I am so proud to be called her Auntie.

She has been my calm in my storms, an ear when I needed someone to talk to, and a person to get advice from when life took me down the dirt roads. She is my biggest critic, making sure I always be the best in everything I do.

I will always cherish the conversations and I anticipate what lies ahead of us. I want you to know I am immensely proud of the woman that you are, and I pray God continues to mold you into the woman you are destined to be. If you continue to put God first, everything will work out.

Your Auntie will always be here to love you, motivate you, and be here when you just want to get things off your chest. This intellectual, strong, and giving woman I am talking about is Brittany Davis. She is my beautiful niece, and I will forever be grateful for her presence in my life. I hope this book makes you smile and gives you what you were trying to pull out of me.

This book is also dedicated to the newest addition to my family, my grandson Myheir Alexander Jamari Myers. I thought I knew what real love was but when I laid eyes on him, my heart just poured with tears. I never knew seeing my grandson for the first time would leave me in tears. He means the world to me and so much more. I want to give him the world and more. He makes me want to change everything about myself and make sure he has everything he needs. I am so thankful for his presence, and I am glad God blessed me with him. He is my calm in the middle of a storm and brings nothing but joy in my life. I will forever be grateful to my daughter Amaani and my future son-in-law Jarrod for bringing such joy into my life.

PROLOGUE

Dear Reader,

First, I would like to take a moment to thank you for purchasing this book. Words will never be able to express just how grateful I am for your support. This journey as an author has not been easy but it has been worth it. I have met new people and been able to release sentiments that were concealed for years. I have experienced moments as an author I never thought I would experience.

Family has always been the most important aspect of my life. I am blessed that I am a part of such a big family. My family is so unique because it is divided in two ways. My mother is the product of the Thompson and Platt families. It was not until I was a teenager when I knew my grandparents existed because my mother was raised by her aunt and uncle.

This was the moment when I found out I was kin to everyone!

My grandparents made sure I knew who my family was by having family reunions or gatherings to get the family together. Although the years I spent were short-lived with them because they passed away, I was grateful to have memories with them. When they passed away the family was not the same. There were no more gatherings to bring the family together.

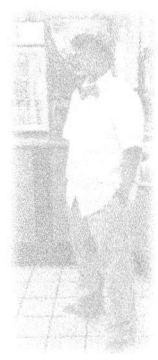

ABOUT THE AUTHOR

Nikki Nicole was born and raised in a small town in South Carolina. She currently resides in North Carolina with her spouse and children. She is the youngest of her siblings on her mothers' side and the middle child of her siblings on her fathers' side.

Her journey as an Author began when she was five years old. She carried around a notebook, pencil, and a book bag everywhere she went. As a teenager she published her first two poems entitled "Tears" and "A True Friend." Although her dreams were to become an Author, she worked in the customer service industry for over twenty years.

After years of collecting her thoughts, she finally stepped out on faith and published her first collection of poetry in 2022 entitled "Family

Ties". By the end of 2022, she published another collection of poetry entitled "Portrait of my Soul". Family Ties and Portrait of my Soul are on display in three libraries, four high schools, a gift shop, a women's shelter, and a museum. In 2023, she published a collection of short stories entitled "Mixed Emotions" and the first series of her autobiography entitled "Camouflaged". Since she has started her journey as an author, she has been a guest on a tv show, a podcast, and spoke at two events at a high school for Black history month and poetry month.

Nikki Nicole has always had a passion to write, and she hopes that her thoughts can help someone or encourage someone in their lives to never give up on their dreams. It is never too late to follow your dreams or be the person you desire to be.

DEAR SELF

Through the years

You have endured tears.

Through the tears

You have experienced heartache and pain.

Yet you still look the same.

People wonder how you made it.

But never questioned why you did not quit.

You stood even when you should have fallen.

Going through everything from Heaven to Hell

How could you smile through it all?

Especially the times when you had no one to call.

Life knocked you down.

But you still claimed your crown.

Even though life is still hard.

You romombor it was nobody but the Lord.

That saved you from you.

Showing you a love, you never knew

Here you are again facing life.

Hoping for a win

But how can you pretend?

That the scars are not there

And the people you loved the most did not care.

How can you stand when you are weak?

Yet you continue to speak.

Where do you go from here?

How can you move without fear?

So many questions to be answered.

But still your prayers are being answered.

Never thought you would be here.

But God has allowed you to move without fear.

It is your time.

It is your moment.

Time to stand.

Time to move.

Even in the moments of fear

Because there is a reason you are here

SEMICOLON

As she sits with tears in her eyes

She wonders how she will rise.

How did she get through the pain this long?

Maybe it was the writing in her notebook or the

words to her favorite song.

Regardless of how she made it.

She still stood through it all.

From one hit to the next hit

Even on the days she had no one to call.

She remained strong even when she was weak.

With no guidance to seek

She took matters into her hands.

Gave into all the demands.

Her back was against the wall.

She just wanted to end it all.

Sitting in the sun

She contemplated about she had done.

All she saw was lights from the ceiling in a place

unknown

She wondered what she was doing wrong.

Now she is getting her stomach pumped from an

overdose.

But God stepped in

Disappointed at the path she chose.

He could not understand why she was not proud of the

skin she was in

The waiting room is filled with family and friends.

Praying God would step in

Finally, she is free.

Maybe this time she will be the woman she needs to

be.

Her life was on pause.

But her purpose still active

It is time for her to accept her flaws.

Attend practice.

Show up and show out.

Claim her spot.

Remember the lessons she was taught.

Hold her head high.

Because God allowed her to still be here

Even when tears fell.

Finally, she is no longer in pain.

But she is prepared to face the rain.

Although life will never be the same

She will never forget to call his name.

RESCUE 9-1-1

Hanging from the cliff

With no direction

Swinging drained with determination

Looking for a lift

No one around

To pull you to the ground

Life still goes on.

Yet you are still the one they call on.

With a single cent

You save them without consent.

Regardless of your circumstances

You still give them a chance.

Now you are wounded.

With a blurred vision

Searching for a way to turn things around.

Hoping there is someone to call.

Then you remember you were the rescue team

Repairing situations and supporting their dreams

Now it is your turn but there is no one to rescue

you.

Is this reality?

Or will someone come eventually?

Finally realizing there is only one person to turn

to

The one you always knew.

Hung on a cross day and night.

Giving you a chance to fight

He was only a call away.

All you had to do was pray.

Because of him you can see

Because of him you are free

PROTECT MY SEEDS

I pray every day.

Lord, please let them make it to another day.

Innocent lives taken too soon.

Leaving broken hearts and empty wounds

One shot changes a life.

Leading to a life filled with nothing but pain and strife.

Is this how life is supposed to be?

Leaving mothers feeling empty

Every day I pray.

God, please teach my seeds to pray.

Give them the courage I never had.

When times are hard, and life treats them badly.

 Made a lot of mistakes.

But I pray that God gives my seeds a break.

Young and old lives lost to violence.

How can we continue to live in silence?

Makes me wonder how Martin Luther King feels.

To know the world never healed

Was his dream in vain?

Will this world ever change?

Or will we be stuck in the shadows of racism?

I pray my children will not be the next victims.

I pray they will stand for something.

And not be penalized for doing nothing.

I am so glad my ancestors fought for us to be freed.

But all I can do is fight to protect my seeds.

It is a cruel world we are living in.

But I wonder how we can defend ourselves.

Our families, friends, and first kin

Judged by the color of our skin.

I could have sworn that was a sin.

When will the fight end?

Or will continue to follow this trend.

Father, please protect my seeds.

Acknowledge their virtuous deeds!

Every day I pray.

Change will come one day.

Is the dream deferred?

Or will our cries be forever unheard.

ANOTHER YEAR, ANOTHER TEAR

Another holiday is here.

Another moment filled with tears.

No more dinners at your house on Thanksgiving

Just memories on repeat I am reliving.

Although you are in my fathers' place

I would give anything just to see your face.

Only if Heaven had a phone.

I would call just to say hi.

I know you are not supposed to question God.

But I cannot help but to ask why.

I remember the day you left me.

It will always be a fresh memory.

I know you are up there cooking a big meal.

Dipping Peach snuff, drinking a Budweiser, and

keeping it real.

I wonder if God knew how much you meant to me.

Would he have chosen you anyways?

I guess he could not resist your sense of humor and

your outspokenness.

Every Thanksgiving the pain will still be here.

I will always yearn for you to be near.

The days will continue to pass by

And I will look up at the sky.

Hoping you are thinking of me too.

Praying God will continue to pull me through

Even though you hurt me with this one.

You will never be forgotten.

Some day we will meet again.

And for once everything will be the same again

WHEN THEY ARE GONE

I remember the days when the family came together.

Now I find myself wondering if things will get better.

Family gatherings have turned into funerals.

No more family reunions

Just random calls of confusion

Unknown disputes and empty rooms

No more Sunday dinners

To unwind from the week

Instead, they just do not speak.

Holding grudges that lead to regrets.

No more holidays filled with love.

Just memories engraved in the sky above.

When the glue that held the family together is no longer here

No one checks on one another.

Everyone is more focused on what they hear.

When they are gone

There is no one left to call on.

Just a faded memory left behind.

A PARENT'S HEART

Sitting up in the middle of the night

Hoping your child is all right.

On your knees asking God for help

Asking for guidance of their footsteps

Pacing the floor

Waiting by the door

Staring at the phone

With an empty dial tone

Hoping they will come home safe.

Keeping the faith

But your heart continues to race.

It continues to race until you see your child's
face.

Visions going through your mind.

Pleading God will send you a sign.

Finally, they are home.

Your thoughts are put to rest.

You have survived another test.

But you will never forget where he brought you from

DEAR DAD,

It has been twenty-eight years since you have gone.

Every day that passes by, I think of you.

Sometimes I wish I could just pick up the phone.

To tell you everything I have been through.

Another Father's Day is here, and I am still in tears.

I thought it would get easier over the years, but the pain continues.

But your memories still live within me.

I just wish you could see your grandson and granddaughter. Nikolaas is tall like you. Amaani is level-headed like you. I just wish it were something I could do to bring you back just one more day, but

I guess I will continue to pray. God gives me strength to see another day. I never expected you to leave so soon, but God needed a plumber for his bathrooms. Words will never express how much I miss you. I will just continue to try to make you proud in every way. Sometimes I wonder how you would feel to know I am gay, but I know you would accept me anyway. I have published two books and I know you are smiling up there to know your only daughter is making something of herself. Well Dad, I had to check in with you like I do every year to let you know I am still here. One day we will meet again and what a day it will be to finally see the person I have been missing again after all these years. Until we meet again Dad, I will continue to reminisce about the memories we had.

WHAT IS FAMILY?

Many times, I have pondered about this question.

Some would say family is everything.

Others would disagree.

But for me family is love, sacrifice, and loyalty.

Sharing unforgettable moments

Swapping secrets

Laughing until tears come to your eyes.

Hosting cookouts with hot dogs and hamburgers on the grill

A safe place to express how you feel.

Family to me is everything plus more.

Holidays filled with joy.

With a table filled with love

Family is sharing, caring, and supporting one another.

Even when times are rough.

Prayers when the Devil is busy.

Words of encouragement on a rainy day

But does family exist anymore?

Or are we just broken links connected by blood?

With no genuine affection

Lost without direction.

Family is so much more than what people say.

It is a feeling that never ends.

Long-lasting friends

A relationship last

A love unmatched

The question remains.

Does family still exist?

Or do we just connect by chains?

Or is our love for another sufficient?

BEHIND THE WALLS

Behind the walls

I feel like nothing at all.

Fake smiles with no invites

Yet they think everything is all right.

Showed up for you.

Just to be rejected by you.

The way you made me feel.

But like always I will heal

May not be a millionaire.

But I am always there.

Life is unfair.

Especially when it comes to the ones you thought

cared.

One day I will rise.

To your surprise

Maybe then you will want to be next to me.

But reality

Is I cared when no one else did.

I was there when no one else showed up.

This is the way things are supposed to be.

Thank God I finally see!

The ones I thought loved me.

Never cared about me

Behind the walls

Nothing is ever the way it seems to be.

It is just the Lord and me

THE BLANKET

You keep me warm.

Through the sunshine and thunderstorms

Although you are filled with many colors

Over the years you seem much duller

You cover me up in the winter.

Your pattern is simple.

Made of cotton

Rarely forgotten.

Easy to carry.

Sometimes temporary

Torn in places.

With limited expectations

Winter is here again.

I cannot wait to cover up with you again.

As I look for you

High and Low

Remembering the moments, I look forward to

Wrapped with you when it is cold.

You felt good when you were bought.

But now you are lost.

A memory in my mind

But for now, you will have to be left behind.

THE TREE

Withstands all storms.

Rain, sunshine, and snow

Thrives in its unique form.

No matter what it continues to grow.

Roots are planted.

But never damaged.

The leaves may fall.

But it still grows tall.

When branches break

You are left weak and wounded.

Yet you are still strong.

But you will not survive.

Without nutrients, food, or water

Through it all you remain strong

Even in places you do not belong

BROKEN GLASS

Not many places will accept you.

You always rejected.

Rarely protected.

You will never return like new.

Over time you will break down

From different temperatures, winds, and storms

Never returning to the same form

You are transparent.

Yet you are still resilient.

Even in your vulnerable state

You are easy to terminate.

When shattered you are a mess.

But you pass every test.

Eventually you will need to be replaced.

But your presence can never be erased.

You may become weak.

But you will still be unique.

FADED JACKET

Green and pink

With a star pattern

A jean texture.

A fabric that is durable

With a missing link

Ripped and worn out.

A little girl's wish.

Filled with stories to tell others about.

The perfect gift on Santa's list

Although it fits the same

It is tied to memories and pain.

A broken heart

But the memories will never depart.

Stained in some places.

Intended to keep you warm.

Protect you from storms.

A shield in good and bad situations

A reminder of a child's imaginations

Faded but everlasting.

BRACELET OF LOVE

Engraved with a name.

With links bonded by love

A gift like no other

From a mother

On the day of birth

The greatest gift of all

Made of silver

A lifetime treasure.

With memories of love

A diamond in the rough

Given from the heart.

A gift to always be remembered.

Kept close to the heart.

With a love that will never depart.

ALL I GOT IS YOU

Lost my father at fifteen.

Years I wished it were a dream.

But God still blessed me with you.

Surviving was all you knew.

Working miscellaneous jobs to make sure I ate.

Teaching me about love and hate

Gave me life in your thirties.

Taught me about bees and birdies.

Had my son at an early age.

But you still made sure I made it to the stage.

Facing days of struggles with a smile

Always taking the extra mile

Praying for a breakthrough

After doing all you could do

Forever grateful for you

Because all I got is you.

LETTER TO MYHEIR

I love you more than you will ever know.

I will you more than I can ever show.

From the top of your head to the bottom of your toes

I will be here for you through it all.

I will be here even if you fall.

I will teach you how to be the perfect gentleman.

How to hold your head high and take a stand.

You will have all the things I never had.

I will be the one you call whether you are happy or

sad.

Grandma will always be here.

Attending basketball and football games

The one in the stand with the loudest cheer

Screaming your name

I will always be just one call away.

With nothing but encouraging words to say

No matter where you are.

Grandma will never be too far.

When life does not treat you fair

I will still be there.

With open arms

WHEN I SEE YOU

A prince is on the way.

Arriving in May

With little hands and small feet

A strong heartbeat

Grandma cannot wait to see you.

Waiting with hugs and kisses just for you

I will hold you in my embrace.

Tell you I love you just in case.

I will teach you everything I know.

And never tell you no

I will give you all of me.

Even if it is falling on one knee.

I will pray for you.

Even when the world turns its backs on you.

Grandma will always be there.

Giving you tender love and care.

Although you are not here yet

I hope you will never forget.

That love was here before you took your first breath.

I will be here when you need to talk.

Even when it is your fault.

I will be here when you need a shoulder to cry on

When you are feeling alone

Grandma will always be here.

Even if it is to shed a tear.

A prince is on the way.

Bright eyed and ready to play.

Born into royalty.

With a world of opportunities

My love and my sunshine

You will be the reason I grind.

My love will be here.

When I see you

I SEE MYSELF IN YOU

From the way you look
To the way you cook
I see myself in You
From the scent of your perfume
To your presence in a room
I see myself in you.
I am who I am.
Because of whom you are ma' am
From the way you walk
The proper way you talk.
I see myself in you.
The over-thinker, seeing things until the end.
To the way you grin
I see myself in you.
Spiritually connected.
Carefully perfected
Stern but kind
A rare jewel to find.
From your mixed gray hair
To the clothes that you wear
I see myself in you.
From the stern look on your face
To the serious looks on your face
I see myself in you.

LEGENDS IN ME

The story begins with a woman of faith.

With a shout that kept a room still

A praying spirit that kept the angels close

With a prayer that traveled from generation to generation

A strength unlike no other

Greatness was instilled in me.

From the moment I opened my eyes to see

With a pencil, notebook, and a destiny

A survival mentality

An armor of protective gear

Whom shall, I fear?

The story continued with a woman with scars.

Touched by an angel.

With an imprint in the stars

An untouchable depository

All because of the legends in me

TO MY FUTURE GENERATIONS

You were born to be great.

You are here for a reason.

You will make mistakes.

But just remember it is your season.

Face the pain

Keep the faith.

Even when you are standing alone in the rain.

Choose your battles.

Not every field is made for war.

Listen even when you cannot hear.

Take charge of your life without fear

Remember success does not sleep.

Never be afraid to leap.

When you fall

Rise with determination

Do not be afraid to crawl.

Remember you determine your destination.

You were created to be great.

But you create your own fate.

Be a catalyst.

Do not just exist!

The world is yours

It is your turn to claim it.

WHEN A FAMILY PRAYS TOGETHER

Imagine how life would be.

If you prayed for me

Imagine if we stood in a circle and held hands.

How much you and I would understand.

When all are united in his name

Everything seems to change.

Family is supposed to be there.

Pray for me if you dare!

Support is not always financial.

But it can beneficial

If you raised your hands to say

Pray for my family!

That they find their way.

Yes, it is easy to say.

But how many of you will take the time to pray?

Everyone is stuck in their way.

When a family prays together

A bond is created forever.

Let our tongue be an asset!

With no regrets

Although feels are never mutual

Until you are sitting at the funeral

Now it is time to pray.

Wishing life were not this way.

Filled with thoughts.

Broken and distraught

When all you had to do was pray

But you chose to push your family away.

Maybe one day everything will get better.

Because the family prayed together

FAMILY FIRST

When you closed your eyes at night

Did you think of me?

Or did you assume everything was all right?

Thought family was supposed to be first.

Guess feelings are just rehearsed.

Love you were the last words you said.

But in my head

I might as well be dead to you.

Longed for relationships that may never happen.

Maybe I am a charity case.

With issues I will never face

Rejected and never protected.

Feeling alone

With an empty dial tone

Who can I call?

When I fall

Family matters

Especially when the world shatters

Truth is when times are hard.

The family flees the scene.

Without a phone call or a card

Feeling like a distant gene

Left to bleed.

Guess love was never guaranteed!

When you are at your worst

Family is never first!

FAMILY IS...

A friend when you need to talk.

Strength when you cannot walk.

A prayer when you cannot speak.

A guidance to seek.

Laughter when you are sad.

Comfort when times are bad.

A hand when you are falling.

Support to your calling

Words of encouragement

A lifetime commitment

Stories of the past

Moments to last

Family is love.

Created from above.

Family is joy.

Even when the Devil comes to destroy.

Family is everlasting memories.

A relationship to last for centuries.

An unbreakable bond

But will this connection be found?

Family is supposed to be a lot of things.

But family only supports you to get ratings.

When the legends are gone

Families fight to belong.

Maybe the damage is already done.

WHY DIDN' T YOU CALL?

Weeks, days, months, and years passed by

Without a phone call

I wondered why.

But I still did not pick up the phone.

I thought maybe you wanted to be left alone.

Now you are flying high.

And all I want to do is cry.

So many good movements shared.

Laughter and waffle house trips

Regardless of the situation, you always showed me you cared.

I wish you knew just how much this hurts.

Now I will never know.

MISSED CALL

Received a call from you.

Never knew this would be the last time I heard from you.

Struck by a car in daylight.

Suspect out of sight.

Left you to die.

Never got the chance to say good-bye.

Wish there were something I could do.

To have a conversation with you once more

God needed you to come home.

To repair and restore souls.

You were an angel on Earth.

With an infectious smile

A vocabulary filled with encouraging words.

Questioned God many times.

Because I never understood

Why did he call you home?

I will never know what you wanted to tell me.

But maybe you were calling to say good-bye.

My heart will forever be in pain.

Your memory will always feel like a fallacy.

Even though your soul is finally free.

WHEN THE HEART SPEAKS

If we were husband and wife

Would you respect our life?

How can you not see you are the reason why?

We cannot see eye to eye.

How dare you stand in the way

Thinking about the things you do is okay.

When does disrespect end?

I guess when the heart is left behind to mend.

Whether you like or not we are kin

With or without you we will still win

Stood before God and a judge to say I do.

Never thought loving me would be an issue.

How could you step in between?

Acting innocent and making a scene

You could have just played your part.

But you chose to dislike me from the start.

How hard is it for you to know your place.

Especially when I have expressed it to your face.

Together we will stand.

When the world turns their backs on us

My homie, lover, and best friend

Through the good, tough times, and even when we fuss.

Finally speaking from the heart

Even though you think none of this is your fault.

Nothing should have to be explained.

But to you it is a game

If the tables were turned

Would you be concerned?

Or act as if you are not the blame?

With no regrets or shame

I am defeated.

Even though your approval was never needed.

When the heart speaks

The strong turns weak

When the heart feels

It slowly heals.

When it comes to me and mine

I will never pay the fine

To be number one

One day you will regret what you have done.

From the heart to the soul

We will never unfold.

I WAITED FOR YOU

Through the heartaches and pain

I never thought things would change.

From one Mr. or Mrs. wrong

To meet the right one.

Never thought a love like yours existed.

But there you were with a love unexpected

Healing a broken heart

Loving me from the start

My first love showed me the way.

Yet she still did not stay.

I was not innocent by far.

But I wish I never had the scars.

Even though I suffered a broken heart.

I still somehow wanted to love again.

I wanted someone to love me the way I loved them.

Then it was you?

Showing me a world, I never knew

Comforting me when times were hard.

Being my biggest supporter

Even when I failed repeatedly.

I am so glad I waited for you.

Because now I know what love feels like

From the early morning conversations

With an unbelievable connection

I know you have wondered several times what I have

gotten myself into

But you stuck around to see my truth.

Every day I am reminded of the person you are.

Sometimes I wonder how we made it this far.

Even though love has taken us to places we never knew.

We continued to fight to see things through.

All because I waited for you.

HEAVEN SENT SOMEONE

Another day has come.

Filled with decisions and issues.

Questioning myself, can I make it?

Will I fail or can I make this work?

I know it was God's grace that I made it this far.

Sleeping in the car

With no food to eat

Hot days in heat

Taking showers at the truck stop

Praying we did not have to deal with the cops.

Looking over our shoulders scared

Wishing someone would have cared.

Working every day

With nowhere to stay

All we could do was pray.

Because we knew God was the only way

Questioning every day why me

Not knowing that God had a plan for me.

Be patient my child is what told me.

Everything will work out eventually.

As days passed by

The more I asked the question why.

Why did I have to go through this?

What did I do to deserve this?

But God knew I was built for this.

He stood by me when I had no one.

Regardless of what I had done.

When the Devil stepped in

God reminded me of where I have been.

He knew I would make it.

He knew I could take it.

Through the storms

I remained strong.

Through the winds

I was reassigned.

All my rainy days turned into sunny days.

My sadness turned into praise.

Suddenly I had a new best friend.

The wind beneath my wings

No more pain

No more rain

Finally, I won.

Because Heaven sent someone

CHAIN OF THOUGHTS

If I could change the person I am

Maybe someone would give a damn.

I was created in his image.

But years of pain did the damage.

Wish I could erase all the mistakes.

But God did not allow me to take breaks.

Walked the journey alone.

Never thought it would take this long.

Started off with a crowd.

But they left me on the ground.

Crawled until I made it.

Never quit.

Everyone has skeletons.

Yet they still throw the first stone.

Fought until success was proven.

Still felt like I was losing.

People show up for fame.

Dismiss you when you are in pain!

Now ain't that a shame

But life does not stop.

Even when you are at the top.

Move in silence is what they say!

But if I had my way

I would turn back the clock.

To change my thoughts!

WHAT WOULD YOU DO?

What would you do If I were not here?

Would you wait for someone to rescue you?

Or pray God will help you?

Could you stand on your own feet?

Or would you let the world defeat you?

Could you breathe on your own without me?

Or would you stand still with a plea?

What would you do if I were not here?

Shed a tear or shake with fear?

If it was you against the world

How would you react?

What path would you take?

Would you be lost or wise?

Or take cover in disguise?

Now is the time to stand?

Forever is not guaranteed.

God is your only friend.

Just let him lead.

Stay strong even in the storm.

Confident, obedient, and faithful

Even when your eyes are full.

When the day comes, and you are alone.

You will still smile and go on

FACES OF DECIET

What face will you show me today?

The real one or the fake one

Loyalty is everything is what they say.

But people are only around when you have won.

Friends come and go.

Even when friendships should mean so much more.

People will pretend to be your friend.

Even your next kin

To use and abuse you.

Just to leave you

When you fall

Avoiding your calls

All because you fell to the ground.

Now the table is turned.

Now everyone wants to be around.

But the bridges are burned.

Maybe next time they will think twice.

Maybe make a sacrifice

Finally made it to the top.

The doors are unlocked.

Look who is there.

The ones that left you in the struggle ready to

claim their share.

No grudge is held.

Just a test failed.

EMPTY PRAYERS

Today I fell to my knees.

Asking God to help me please.

I asked him to keep me.

But sometimes I wonder if it is just a fallacy.

I know he sits high and looks low.

But sometimes I wonder if he really knows.

The pain I have endured.

Does he see the open wounds?

From this moment to the womb

Does he hear my cries?

Or are my feelings disguised?

Yet I still rise.

With a hustle and grind on my mind

Hoping to find

The best version of me

Because I know my prayers are not empty

I AM SORRY

Three words people rarely use.

Some mean it, some just say it.

Three words that are always abused.

Most people will never admit it.

Three words that can change or save a life.

But at what price

Three words that are hard to say.

Yet people still misuse it every day.

Why is it so hard to admit when you are wrong?

Are you afraid it will make you weak?

But I guess everyone should just play along.

And turn the other cheek.

Three words that could change the world.

Or become a lesson learned.

Guess I am sorry is not for everybody.

QUESTIONS

Why do people treat people the way they do?

Maybe it is because they forgot the golden rule.

Treat others the way you wanted to be treated.

Just to end up blocked without a clue.

Why don't people say what they feel?

Instead, they pretend to be real.

Why don't people show love while you are here?

They just wait until the funeral to shed a tear.

Why do people pretend to love you?

But the whole time they are gossiping about you.

Plotting against you

Why do people say they will be there?

Pretend to care.

But disappear when the struggle is real.

Praying on your downfall

Hoping they are not the person you call.

So many questions to ask.

While repairing relationships that were never meant
to last

So many questions lie helplessly in the back of my mind.

But who knows, maybe this is a sign.

A WORLD WITHOUT LOVE

Stuck in a world where love is not there.

Forced to love another person is not fair.

Love should have been there.

Even when life did not treat me fairly.

You do not belong here.

The words I feared.

Heaven or Hell is a choice.

But what about my voice?

Worried about what the world sees.

Instead of paying attention to how things should be.

In the back of my head are the lessons I was taught

Battles I fought.

Do I belong here?

Hoping the feelings would disappear.

Cannot believe a four-letter word.

Left me with words unheard.

Stuck in a world of sin.

No one cares about where I have been.

Never changed who I am.

Only changed the paths I took.

Gave a hundred percent.

But love was never present.

Stuck in a world where love never existed.

Wishing someone would have just listened.

A LOVE I ONCE KNEW

Tired of being last

When I should be in first place

Instead, my heart is shattered like glass.

Yearning for your embrace

Maybe your feelings are not the same.

Or your heart has changed direction.

But I must admit I am tired of playing this game.

Lacking attention

Praying for a better situation

But I am still patiently waiting.

Reminiscing of the days we were dating.

Praying for a resolution

But love is a strong emotion.

Yet I am still captivated by your motion.

From the way you walk

To the beautiful tone in your voice

Leaving me with no choice

You are my lover and best friend.

Even when we are standing at a dead end.

Can you open your heart?

Love me the way you did from the start.

Or will this love fade?

With regrets about the decisions, we made.

Love me once more.

Remember the reason we wanted more.

Love for you is beyond definition.

Yet we are stuck in another dimension.

Can we travel to the place we once knew?

Or will we continue to be trapped in a place we never knew?

Let us remember the time.

And get it right this time.

I WANT YOU AROUND

If I could press rewind

To before you were mine

I would take my time.

To get to know you.

Love you more.

Hold you more.

If we could just start all over again

To right our wrongs

My soul cries for you

My heart whispers your name

Just the thought of you takes my breath away.

For years I yearned for you

Whispered a prayer to God above to find someone like
you.

One conversation led to you and me.

Walking down the aisle to our destiny

Finally, my heart is free.

My soul is at peace.

Because I found everything in you

TEARS OF AN ANGEL

Your bags were packed by the door.

You just did not know your destination.

You heard someone call your name.

But at the time you did not know who it was

When you woke up, you did not recognize anyone.

You wondered where everyone had gone.

But you were so excited about your new home.

Finally, you had everything you wanted and needed.

You were finally able to meet your father.

But this did not stop you from missing your loved

ones.

You wanted to visit your old home one more time.

Just to tell everyone goodbye

Even though you are in a better place.

You cannot help but shed tears.

Because everything that mattered to you was not there

You wanted to share the experience with the ones you

loved most.

But God chose you to come live in his house.

It is everything you imagined and so much more.

From the moment you walked in the door

You could see the finer things in life.

Now this is the life you could get used to

It is so much to do.

Golden gates, golden paved roads, and healthy plates

You even saw a few people you once knew.

As you look down from Heaven hoping someone will hear

your cry

Asking God why

Why did I have to leave them behind?

His response was, "you are one of a kind."

If you had one more moment to say I love, you.

One more moment to tell everyone you love them.

You finally won the race.

You were finally in the right place.

For now, it is good-bye.

But one day you will be reunited.

And you will not have to cry.

LOOKING DOWN FROM HEAVEN

The time has come to say good-bye.

I finally get to tell my dad, Grandparents, and Aunt

Wees hi.

My bags were already packed.

My outfit was already picked out.

I tried to prepare you.

But God said there was nothing I could do.

I wish I did not have to go.

But here is where my ink no longer flows.

I have had some good and tough times.

Even wrote a few rhymes.

But when God calls you

You must leave behind everything you once knew.

Some will be sad, and some may cry.

Some will question why.

I have lived my life.

Had a beautiful wife.

Kids and a mother that loved me.

Even walked across the stage to get my degree.

Now God says it is time to go.

Taking me to a place I have never seen before.

I know you are wondering if I am in Heaven or Hell

But only my heart will tell.

As I look down from Heaven

I see the Reverend.

Giving a powerful message ending with a YEAH

The choir is singing one of my favorite songs DELIVER
ME

As I look down from Heaven

I am casket sharp.

Dressed in a button up with a bow tie.

I am waving good-bye.

Please do not worry about me.

Because God will take care of me

As I look down from Heaven

It is well with my soul.

I have brand new clothes.

I have claimed my crown.

On the road Heaven bound

With a new name

And a new address to claim.

THANK YOU FOR YOUR SUPPORT

I WOULD LIKE TO TAKE A MOMENT TO THANK YOU FOR PURCHASING THIS BOOK. THIS JOURNEY HAS NOT BEEN EASY BUT IT HAS BEEN WORTH IT. BECAUSE OF YOU I HAVE CONTINUED TO TELL MY STORY AND BECAUSE OF YOU I WILL CONTINUE TO MAKE MY DREAMS COME TRUE. I HOPE THIS BOOK INSPIRES YOU TO REACH OUT TO YOUR FAMILY, CHECK ON ONE ANOTHER, BE THERE FOR ONE ANOTHER, PRAY FOR ONE ANOTHER, AND DO NOT WAIT UNTIL THE FUNERAL TO LET SOMEONE KNOW YOU LOVE THEM. CONTINUE TO BE BLESSED! IF YOU WOULD LIKE AN ADDITIONAL COPY, PLEASE VISIT WWW.NIKKINICOLE.ORG.